Want More?
Just Start.

Janny Tolman

Janny Tolman

Enjoy, pass on
for More abundance!
Dream!

6-30-2024

Book Cover by Kevin and Jennifer Poulson

Illustrations by Janny Tolman

This book is dedicated to
YOU!

To you for picking it up and
choosing to put yourself
first.

To you as you love yourself
and start this next step in
your journey.

Give yourself a pat on the
back.

Let's go!

"I would recommend this educational & spiritual book to anyone who battles with self worth or love. Janny has shared some proven secrets and techniques to unlocking the key to our own hearts and learning how to be comfortable in our own skin. Thank you for reminding me that true love starts from within." – Erica Cooper, EFDA, current patient

"This story - Janny's story - inspires the reader with nuggets of impactful and practical insights for living a life of genuine self love." – AJ Mitchell, Esq.

"There is a beautiful balance of the scientific and the spiritual which is so much needed in today's world. They are woven together intricately and seamlessly in this well-written and heartfelt work of art." – Angie Debing, M.Ed., B.A, 29 years teaching

"Janny does a beautiful job of sharing her journey, and takes it a step further by teaching how the brainstem was involved in being able to make the changes she needed to make. She has connected her spiritual voyage with physiology. Using the two, this little book could be the tool to help you make big changes." – Dr. Bill Gallagher, D.C.

Contents

Chapter 1

Would you like to take a walk with you?

There was a time I was running so fast, doing so much, taking care of everything and everyone. I was a million miles ahead of any feeling, making it impossible to truly go deep inside and feel the pain. The pain was too great, the feelings too much, so I ran. I ran in every good way, spreading joy for all to feel and see, thereby masking my pain with much-needed happiness. The deep feelings stayed buried right there inside of me.

There was a deep pain I didn't even know existed and I had no idea I was running from. I did so very many good things. However, I lived with a heart deeply wounded and bleeding with sorrow that was unknown to me as I ran. I stayed miles ahead of the pain, that while I would feel it occasionally to its depth, for the most part all I felt were twinges of sadness.

Until that changed. Until the pain grew. Until my old methods no longer were enough. Until I needed to breathe and no longer could. I tried to run. If I ran faster, farther than ever before - I would reach the top. But this was not true.

I was given the opportunity to sit and listen to my psychologist tell me details of the path, my path, laid out before me – the path to begin to have changes in my life. This journey as described would be long and arduous. It made no sense the length of this new direction, for I had always been able to fix things and mind you - fix them rather quickly. A decision was made to embark down the path. What I learned as I walked, what I learned in my healing journey, I would like to share. My invitation to you - want more? ...just start.

There came a day when I sat before my psychologist, this man possessing caring, knowledge and candor when he told me bluntly, "I cannot help you progress further if you cannot slow down." I declared with certainty that I had indeed slowed my mind, my life – yes my brain had slowed down. Of note, he was not with me every day, so what does he know? I would show him as I set my intention when I spoke with him to speak S-L-O-W-L-Y. Looking back I can see how clear it was I had NOT slowed down and he was accurate in his astute assessment.

Have you ever had the opportunity to look back on a time, back on experiences and just sit in awe at the miraculous puzzle being worked in your life? For the miracles, the circumstances, everything that was orchestrated for me in my life, it is no coincidence. I would be remiss if I failed to share what was clearly given to me, a humble student full of insatiable thirst for knowledge. I saw how loved I am, how cared for I am, how gifts being given to me are gifts resulting from the journey I was given and the journey I ultimately chose.

Right at this time I had the fantastic opportunity to begin training to study cranial nerves and injuries, healing and helping others heal. My phenomenal teacher and skilled practitioner knew of the difficulty to guide others towards healing from a place of brokenness or lack so off we went to find ourselves, to heal our heart, mind, body and soul. We were taught the power of the body, specifically the cranial nerves, and what our mind can do. (Cranial nerves, something I knew very little about – these important nerves send the signals from your brain throughout your body.) We have the tools inside of ourselves, every tool we need. Will you begin the walk?

Chapter 2

Cannot do more or be more

I want to do MORE. I demand MORE. I cannot do more. BUT WAIT!?! Did you say cannot do more? Yes, that is correct. Cannot do more. Well where does that leave me if I cannot do any better? What am I supposed to do if in this moment I am unable to do better?

Stick with me here because this is important. It leaves me EXACTLY where I am supposed to be. It allows me to accept this moment, this challenge, this situation, this place. It allows for acceptance. Trust me as we work through doubts, it allows for unlimited hope.

It is possible your brain is asking questions too fast for the answers to come, so let's take this a thought at a time. Just because you CANNOT do what you want, be what you want exactly right now, does not mean you are not headed in the perfect direction with exactly the right tools you need for right now AND all of the answers you desire on the horizon.

Breaking it down – you did not CHOOSE this place. You did not choose so much of your life. Life, fear, generational patterns, uncontrollables all played a big role in bringing you here.

Did you wake up when you were three years old and say, "You know what? I am going to make my life into the biggest mess I possibly can! I am going to make intentional choices that will ruin everything and that is exactly what I want!" Did you ever at any point wake up at any age and say this to yourself? Of course you did not.

This amazing brain of yours is designed for survival and survive it will, often at the expense of your peace and happiness. Throw aside whatever is unnecessary - to SURVIVE. Fight or flight or freeze. Run from the bear. Get to safety.

Please understand there is work ahead. It will take work to undo what has been done so that "cannot" is no longer reality for the pieces you desire. Based on what you have been through, your subconscious programming, your fight or flight, in this moment you cannot simply unprogram everything with a magic wand.

So buckle up, get ready for ups and downs, because it will be a bumpy ride. You will be with YOU every step of the way. Feel the excitement run from your head all the way to your toes filling each part of you with anticipation that this ride you and you (yes you read that correctly – you get to travel with you!) are embarking on will be the ride of your life!

What do I need you to accept, believe and surrender? This is important. This will help you each time you want "more". You cannot just DO better. You cannot willpower it away, faith it away, pray it away. The brain stem will win. Cranial nerve 5 will keep you in fight or flight or fright or holy crap.

(Brief definition - Cranial nerves are located in the brain, called cranial nerves because they emerge from the cranium. They have sensory and motor components. They have areas of voluntary and involuntary control. Cranial nerves are foundational powerhouses controlling functions in the body and sending signals throughout the body. They can be damaged or impaired through physical, emotional and mental trauma causing various problems. They can be activated to enable necessary functions and modalities.)

Once we accept the possibility it is true, that we cannot just do better and neither can anyone else, especially when we are in fight or flight, now we are ready to begin change. With the engagement of our parasympathetic nervous system we begin to activate peace, calm and acceptance.

Have you ever heard the word regret or apologize and felt shame and guilt? Or fear and judgement? Understand that in these moments the best was given and there is no shame because you did the very best you were capable of in that moment. The path before you is simply to BEGIN to change. To keep a path of metanoeo (a Greek word) – change mind, knowledge, spirit, breath!

Here I sit without judgement, guilt, shame or sadness. I sit with hope. I am full of hope, for I have done the best I can in each moment. Often the best I could do was nothing I am excited about, brag about or would share with ease. I do understand that it truly was for me in that moment my best and I COULD NOT do any better.

I know my heart. I know I want more. I know my desires. Knowing this, if I could have done better, I would have done better. So I accept from a place of love each moment of my life.

My excitement rises as I see a future where I can do better and I will do better. What does that look like? What am I doing? How do I feel? I want to know and feel it now! So I refuse to wait for life to be perfect in order for me to feel amazing. I get to teach my brain what it feels like to live the life I want to live and respond the way I want to respond to situations. I give myself a new memorized emotion of peace, joy, happiness.

The things that I could not do and right now cannot do, I WILL be able to do. This is where hope and power lie.

So, will you give this time? Will you enjoy the journey to discover? If you choose to say yes, you will understand transformation in a way that is indescribable. You will want to sing from the rooftops in joy. Who really does that anyway? Well we should, right?!

Because – you will never want this journey to end.

Each time you see with awareness that you did your best and you could not do any better in that moment, you will look forward with excitement seeing change is on the horizon, beauty is in the present and miracles are in store.

You, my friend walk with you. You face your fears. You choose love. In doing so, your walk is with clarity, a walk with your higher self, with your true you – nothing masked.

There was a time I was my drill sergeant. Any mistake I made it seemed to be time to use condemnation and shame as I beat myself up mercilessly over what I had done, with little or no forgiveness. Then as I held myself to this standard, I began to hold all those I loved to this impossible standard of demands, performance, integrity, whatever I felt was necessary to BE. Little did I know that we could NOT do better.

You might be thinking – well is this a free pass to mess up, be lazy, not care and just declare, "I could not do any better!" This is what our fear tells us. The fear continues with the thought that if we accept that we cannot do any better in that moment then we will stop trying, so we have to be hard on ourselves if we want any kind of improvement. Our brain tells us that if we allow ourselves space to just be, then we will truly fail.

Instead, with love, we choose to thrive. We choose to step up because we want to. We are not running or afraid but we simply want to thrive. We choose more. We give those we care for space to show up, space to choose more, space to grow and change. Space.

The hopeful part of this – I want to share with excitement that what I "cannot do" HAS changed. It has improved dramatically. Previously, I could not stop myself from a quick reply, just reactive to someone who said something unkind. I now observe my brain was protecting me from pain, from death, all survival. Now, I have retrained my brain. My brain knows it is safe as I remind it daily. I have time to respond rather than react.

This change has taken work and time and tools and love. It is not a process that is complete nor will it be, but it is a drastic difference, this gift I have given myself to thrive. I have learned. I show up better. I continue to love myself when I cannot do better, when I cannot be more. I love myself for all I am, all the beauty that is me!

Discover JOY in the Journey NOW

“ METANOEO

Change
Mind
Knowledge
Spirit
Breath

Chapter 3

Safety

So what does that mean – for my brain to feel and know it is safe? These are survival skills. We want safety. The basics of safety. When we feel a lack of safety we have fear. I knew this was going on with me. My brain was not safe.

What wasn't I safe with? The answer is so very much. There were things that on the outside might not appear to cause alarm, but I had not taken care of me. It was time to show up better for me, time to be better. Absolutely time to let my brain know! The hard wiring that had taken place needed to be undone.

I like to picture workers digging out the deep grooves that will eventually be a massive freeway of cars traveling to their destinations. Once it is dug, built and paved, traveling is smooth, and full of ease. The cars feel comfortable traveling this path… until they realize they are headed to the wrong destination. The new destination I want to travel to does not have a freeway, yet.

Not only do we need to fill in that old well-worn path, but we want to create a new path. I see the excitement in where this path will take me. I feel the strength I will gain as I dig, build and pave the path I now choose, rather than the path that seems to have just been there. One shovel full at a time, digging a little more each moment, each hour, each day, to travel this new path, knowing it takes time to dig this all out.

I began talking straight to my brain stem, getting straight to the subconscious programing. My cranial nerves love me and are trying to save me and help me. This subconscious programming is in place for protection. Cranial nerve 5 (the trigeminal nerve that connects to the entire body quickly turning on the fight or flight response) has an important job to do which is all about keeping me safe. If a memory tells me there is danger, it is once again time to run.

Here is an exercise I was taught. (Thank you to Lois Laynee with Restorative Breathing!) My eyes are open. I have a stick between my teeth. (The stick between the teeth is to block the clenching of the teeth that turns on the fight or flight response, which sends the message to the 5th cranial nerve that there is an emergency.) Next, I wiggle my toes, rub my hands together (I do this so my brain can see and feel that we are in the present moment) and keeping that stick between my teeth, I look forward into the beauty that is before me and say out loud with clarity "I am 100% safe". I say it again and again and again. After I say it out loud I breathe in through my nose, feeling the peace. Then I hum to allow calm through my entire body. I hear it, say it, feel it, know it – safety. Once my hum wears out, I simply swallow, taking as long as I need for this to occur.

I decided I wanted to see this message with my eyes, sending this communication to my brain, each time I turn on my phone. I wrote in my own handwriting that I am 100% safe and made it the screensaver on my phone, constantly reminding me, retraining me – I am 100% safe. Now I give my brain this message about anything and everything it needs to feel safe with. Examples include: I am 100% safe driving, I am 100% safe being alone and I am 100% safe putting my needs first.

I learned this feeling of safety. I learned that it is not 1976. I am not alone at a baby sitter's house for the weekend, to me a strange place where I don't know if my parents are ever coming back. It is not 2013 and I am not in a horrible car accident. I am not arguing with someone or defending myself. There is not a police officer pounding on my door. I am not crying or feeling alone. I am not sixteen waiting for hours by the phone for the boy I like to call me. Rather, I am 100% SAFE! My brain knowing, truly knowing, so I say it again and again and again. I see it. I feel it. I hear it. All of my cranial nerves get the message.

I now want to feel this all through my body, to pour it through every part of me. I state with confidence that I truly and completely forgive myself, trust myself, love myself - deeply and completely. What does that look and feel like? To do this deeply and completely? How would you feel if you truly and completely loved yourself? Deeply and completely felt 100% safe? Feel it now. I feel it with every part of me! I am full of amazing desires, of beauty, of joy and deep capacity.

I have made mistakes that to me are unforgiveable, or... were unforgivable. I have learned to sit with that moment, the moments my brain works so hard to protect me from. My brain used fear, stress and panic. I sit with the feeling, the mistake. I meet my heart. I see who I desire to be. I feel my heart, my desires. I release shame, blame. I deeply and completely forgive me.

With a stick between my teeth, I say "I am 100% safe" and I feel it. I breathe, hum and swallow and I feel... me. I let my whole brain know this process is truly happening. It does not serve me well to live with this pain. There is nothing to fear. We are releasing this pain.

I wrap myself in unconditional love. There are no conditions I need to meet to be worthy of my love and my forgiveness. I tell myself that I will forgive me every time. I let myself know there is nothing I can do that I will not forgive me for. I let myself know that I deeply and completely trust me. I say to myself, "Janny, I got your back."

Write your name on following line.

_____ I got your back.

When I sit with this emotion, it is simple, pure and beautiful. Life presents opportunities to forget my newfound safety. I become stronger and more capable each time I choose to come back to feeling and knowing 100% safety, to deeply and completely trust myself, forgive myself.

Sometimes I forget and travel the old path. I choose to come back to this new path. I tell myself that I deeply and completely trust myself to return to this feeling. I deeply and completely trust myself to know that I am always 100% safe.

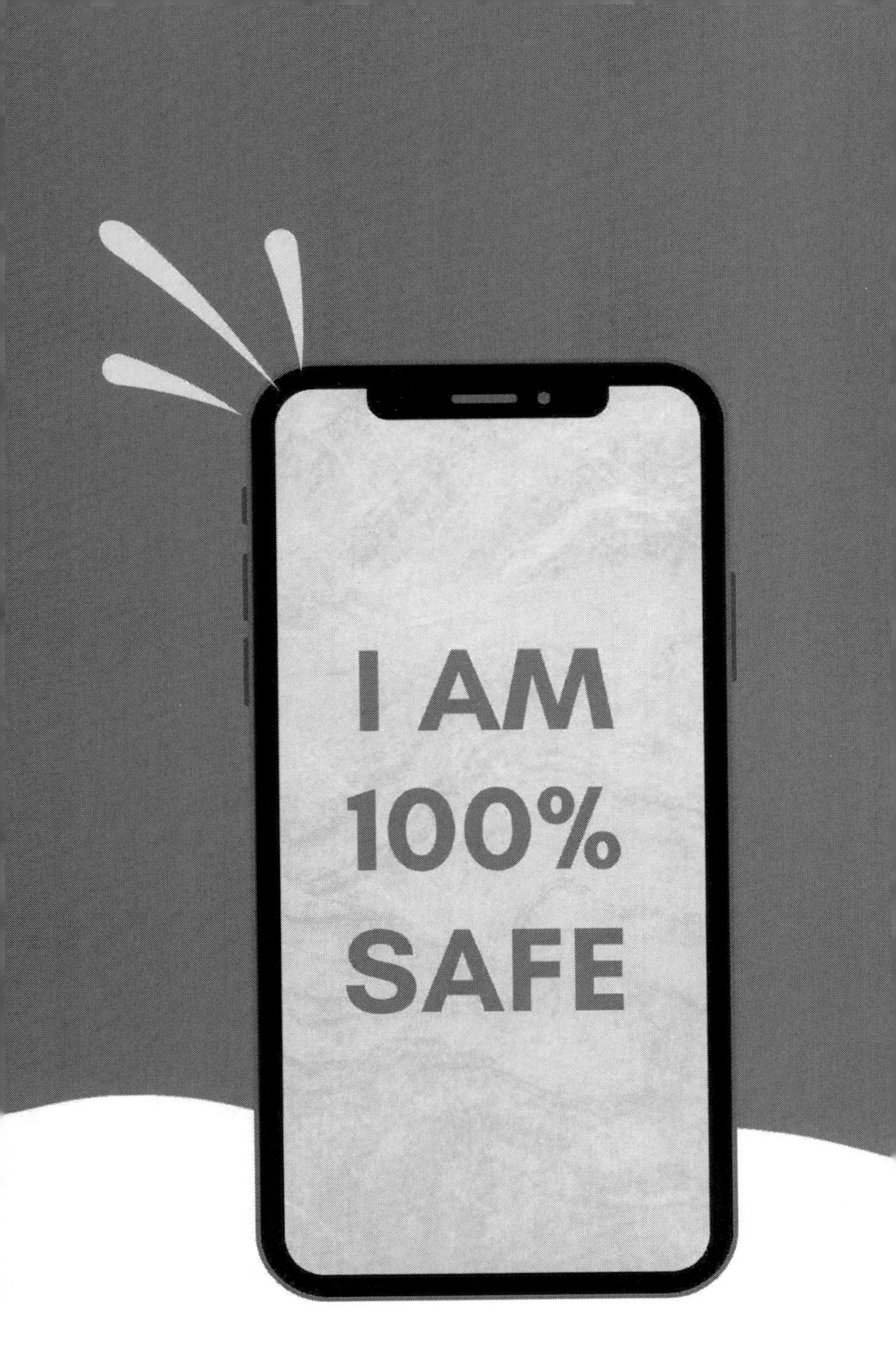
I AM
100%
SAFE

1-PREPARE
Place a popsicle stick between your front four teeth

2-LOOK
Eyes are open focused on one point

6-END
When hum ends swallow. Repeat with any self chosen words

100% SAFE

5-BREATHE
Breathe in through nose then breathe out and hum

3-FEEL
Rub your hands together the entire time

4-SPEAK
Say out loud with stick between teeth- I AM 100% SAFE!

Chapter 4

Turn on the parasympathetic nervous system

The training and practicum that fell in my lap and I jumped at the opportunity to be a part of was with Restorative Breathing. It was run by the CEO and founder, Lois Laynee. This practicum of healing and learning had tools and science I would only even begin to explore! I credit this chapter to Lois Laynee, a brilliant teacher with amazing natural gifts and understanding of the brain. It is shared through my version of how my brain interpreted the information and worked towards healing.

Something critical I learned in the practicum- the sympathetic nervous system has got to be off and then the parasympathetic nervous system can be turned on. Parasympathetic needs to be engaged. I could not go forward with the limbic system running the show, with fight or flight having a field day. So I was taught how to turn it on. Game changer for me. (Just to remind us the sympathetic nervous system is a network of nerves that activate the fight or flight response in the body. The parasympathetic nervous system is the network of nerves that relaxes the body after stress or danger. The parasympathetic nervous system also helps with essential body functions when you feel safe and relaxed.)

What I discovered the first time I did single nasal breathing and added in a four-step connection mind body exercise that I was given to do in a training, was that my whole body felt ready for sleep. The next moment struck me with powerful emotion when tears streamed down my face as I was told, my body has been programmed to either be full steam ahead or off. No in between. Never slow down even to feel, to breathe, to be. Life had been about becoming, and become I will, or die trying! NO LONGER.

How do we get in touch? It is simple. No one is watching you do the following breathing exercises and thinking you are strange – or if they are, then they might want to get strange pretty quickly too! 'Cause I found out that this has got to be on. This foundation for all healing enabled me to begin. A foundation that is necessary for all of the beauty that will follow. As you know, without a solid foundation, sooner or later everything crumbles.

The vagus nerve is a powerful cranial nerve traveling through our body capable of sending messages of healing and calm. Many of the cranial nerves work together for our body to be in a natural state of calm. To feel, know, believe that there is not a threat and we can go into rest and digest, heal and calm mode. What if we could actually live in this place? What if this became our normal state – to feel present, to feel peace?

Single nasal breathing activates the parasympathetic nervous system, which is possible only when the sympathetic (fight or flight) is turned off, making the first step of this exercise the most critical. The first step requires the use of a "block" to the sympathetic nervous system. Grab a popsicle stick and place it between the front four teeth in your mouth so that the ends are sticking out each side. I am not clenching with my teeth, gritting on the stick. Rather the stick simply creates space as I rest my lips on the stick. (Depending on your jaw, you might want to have two sticks or even three stacked on top of one another for a relaxed bite.)

This tool is invaluable. Any time we try to calm our mind and heart, if the teeth are clenched, cranial nerve 5 will win – and win it shall as when we need fight or flight, this is essential. (Cranial nerve 5 remember is the fight or flight nerve that shuts down everything non-essential and turns on what is needed to handle an emergency!) If you don't have a stick then bring your tongue forward slightly to place it between your front teeth. Gratefully, no matter when you need it, you always have your tongue to place between your front teeth. Before I explain the rest, when do we need this tool?

Imagine an emergency, let's keep it simple. Pretend you have a two-year-old son and he is running to the street to get his ball and a car is coming. You see all this before you and what does your body do? Everything goes into fight or flight. We have an emergency and our body needs to respond and knows how to respond. Shut down all non-essential functions. Clench the teeth, grasp for air, save the world! We are so blessed to have the sympathetic nervous system on point. You are there, responding faster than you thought possible, and you are holding your son in your arms.

Soooooo… now we need to turn it off. But how can we? If we rest, if we dial it down, if we are not on high alert – everything could go wrong! Not only could it go wrong, but it will! He could run to the street again, or worse a bomb could hit your home and you have not found a way to have protection! Our brain is sending our body messages to stay in fight or flight, to be on high alert, to keep our energy in panic mode.

We live in a world of go, go go, where there "is" a moment of panic seemingly around every corner. The car behind you is honking, you need gas and might run out! You are late for work, you are out of milk when you just poured your cereal bowl, there is nothing made for dinner, no clean underwear and your HOA says you have to mow your lawn or there will be a fine. Clearly these are the small sympathetic problems. Imagine your alcoholic mother, you lost your job, the 50 pounds you gained since you had your baby causing you to have diabetes and the doctor saying that you will die from cancer. You have a horrible migraine and are suffering from chronic pain that never relents. The list goes on and on.

In March of 2020 many had a chance to experience the opportunity to see what a world could look like if we just slowed down. If things slowed down – completely, if we are not in panic mode. Was it hard to let your life slow down? Were you able to allow it or did you stay in fight or flight?

We see clearly our body and mind have the ability to turn on panic mode. Do we see our body and mind have the ability to turn on the parasympathetic nervous system? We have got to first grab all that energy that is trying so hard to go to fight or flight. Teeth cannot touch. If your teeth are touching, stress wins every single time! Stress wins when necessary, which is a very good thing. Very thankful when I need immediate energy, I can clench my teeth.

What if I am living in a physical and mental state where I am always stressed, where I never rest and digest? I am clenched all night long. Then I live in this charged state constantly and my body is always exhausted as it lives in fight or flight.

Much of the time, we head down a path of stress and worry unnecessarily. With the sympathetic nervous system turned off, we are now ready to learn the rest of single nasal breathing. I use it daily, many times a day. My sympathetic nervous system still tries to run the show and is successful sometimes! I feel a desire to breathe, hum and swallow and my brain will literally demand that I stay in fight or flight. WHY? Because my dear brain loves me and does not want that BAD thing to happen again. Time to get on board – we have work to do and it isn't time to let the brain go off on a journey of every possible fear.

Time to turn on the parasympathetic nervous system. I love the vagus nerve. My daughter-in-law with her degree in medical microbiology remembered the vagus nerve in her studies because it is my favorite! Turn it on. Learn to live here.

How? Here is where we use that stick between the teeth, the front four teeth top and bottom. Keep your eyes open and find a gentle focus, looking ahead at something your eyes and mind feel peaceful with. Breathe in through your nose slowly and silently, filling your lungs with oxygen. Then hum as long as your hum keeps going with a steady sound. When you are done humming, keep the stick between your teeth, keep your eyes open and swallow when ready. Wait for your swallow if needed.

This entire powerful tool we want for your right side of the brain and the left side of the brain. So let's cover one nostril gently by placing the pad of your thumb under one nostril. Repeat this process with the stick, breathe, hum and swallow three times on each side, meaning three times with one nostril covered and then three times with the other.

When you are ready, add the power of the first cranial nerve and get something to smell. I love using my netistick (search for Himalayan Chandra netistick aromatherapy inhaler) that has many calming essential oils in it. I breathe in the smell three times each side, simply adding the smell to the whole single nasal breathing process.

I began to do this, many times a day. I am a different person than I was four years ago. Has it been that long? Has it been that short? I have only had this tool for four years? Now my vagus nerve gets to play! My parasympathetic nervous system is allowed to be a part of the show when I am awake! It fought so hard for space and rarely was heard.

Study all you can to learn all about the parasympathetic nervous system, the cranial nerves, drink it all in, OR – simply trust those who have studied - and apply this simple tool to begin your day, end your day and throughout your day. What would your life be like if you lived in peace and calm? What would your life look like if you did not have underlying constant stress?

Single Nasal Breathing

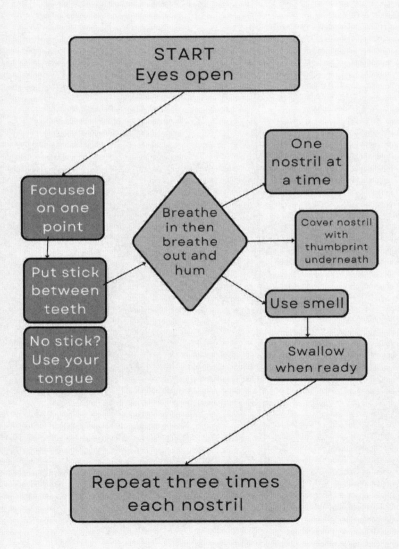

START
Eyes open

One nostril at a time

Focused on one point

Breathe in then breathe out and hum

Cover nostril with thumbprint underneath

Put stick between teeth

Use smell

No stick? Use your tongue

Swallow when ready

Repeat three times each nostril

Chapter 5

Love myself

I get to wake up with me! Each day I get to wake up with me! Sleep with me, hike with me, drive with me, eat with me, dance with me, go on vacations with me, play with me, pray with me. There is no one I would rather be with than me. No one. No one I would rather enjoy the sunset with, sing a song with, listen to their thoughts or just sit with. ME.

This was not always the case. I was doing my 12 step program for the first time. (If you haven't ever had the opportunity, this journey was phenomenal for me to work the 12 steps – think of AA, codependents anonymous etc.) I was on the 4th step when I realized that I am the source of my pain. I blamed myself for anyone who had ever hurt me or any pain I had experienced because I am the one who allowed it. I realized in that moment not only did I not love myself but I hated myself. There was no one to blame but me for all the pain I had experienced in my life. In tears - feeling mentally, emotionally, physically and spiritually drained - I had nothing left and I fell asleep unable to process another moment, thought or feeling.

This beautiful, incredible girl was disliked, even hated by herself.

Years later I would say to a friend when we were out at a bar – there is no difference between me and any other girl in this place except this - the reason guys are asking me to dance is because of my confidence, as they see that I love myself! This was four years after my moment of hatred, four years of work digging in and changing. Years of effort doing the most sacred work any of us will ever do – falling in love with, deeply in love with, the person in the mirror. This is a humble beautiful love. A love based on pure joy, joy knowing that my Heavenly Father created me. He did a phenomenal job and certainly brought His "A" game the day He created me.

I have pure bliss that I get to share each day with me, humbly walking with me. How did I get here? Where did it begin? I implemented a few simple steps from the book "Love Yourself Like Your Life Depends on It". I had these prerecorded programs in my brain that played messages I was not even aware were going on.

I intentionally set a new recording. The recording I chose with guidance from this book was "I love you Janny" and it became the mantra that played and played in my brain day in and day out. I felt it. I breathed it in. On days when I could not feel the beauty this truth provided, I simply said it again and again knowing eventually I would feel it. I looked into the mirror, looking deeply into my eyes to tell me that I love me! Just staring with passion into my inner little girl, my wounded girl, my baby girl, every part of me being filled with love.

I learned by looking in my eyes that deep inside is where my inner child lies. A dear friend taught me how to find her. My baby girl had been through so much pain and she wanted to be safe. When she was ready and when she trusted me she could come out from under the chair, let go of her knees and be free. She wanted to trust me and it was time. I showered myself with love and in doing so, showered my inner child with love.

My kids loved to tease me as I went on a date with myself. Me and me got ice cream, went out to eat, watched movies and went on walks. Me and me took bubble baths, chose our favorite music and hiked to the top of the mountain. I love you Janny.

My psychologist had prepared me for this, to take care of me. He gave me an assignment that I was to adhere to with strictness and rigor: To have 20 minutes of fun a day for the rest of my life. What does fun look like to you?

20 MINUTES OF FUN!

EVERY DAY FOR THE REST OF YOUR LIFE!

What is fun to me, a person who has not deeply loved herself and rarely put herself first? What do I love? What makes my heart sing with joy? It cannot be something that makes someone else happy and you watch them and feel happiness. Oh no – this is me! This is my happiness. I need to feel that happiness through all of me.

I loved to lay on my bed as a girl getting lost in a story, Trixie Belden mysteries. Now I always have a book next to my bed to allow my mind the journey of reading! I love to dance, alone or with someone else. I love to hike. I love to play the piano. I love a good movie! The list grew.

I know how to have fun alone and with others. Each and every day my heart is set free to sing, live and love me! My love affair grew. This fun became a planned part of my day, intentional, me planning to spend time with me, to give my heart the chance to sing and soar each day. My youngest son would tease me – so mom, who are you going on a date with? Yourself again? Who will open the door for you on your date with yourself? When we were vacationing in Newport Beach, CA he encouraged me to take a nice walk on the beach with myself and to hold my hand. Guess what? I might have just done that!

I almost cannot walk past a mirror now without having a mini love affair with me. Without looking at me, into my eyes and seeing me, with excitement declaring my love for me. In the same book about loving myself, I read the concept - why can't we walk down the street with that pep in our step and joy in our heart because we are IN LOVE with OURSELVES!

It is truly a privilege to be me. I am in awe that I get to be me. That I have this opportunity to – be me. Tears come to my eyes as I feel me. As I know me. My heart, my desires, my passions, my excitement, my pain, my joy, my compassion, my thoughts, my feelings, my vulnerability, my weakness and my acceptance. The journey to get to know me is endless.

I realize through this ability to love me that getting to know me is more fun that anyone I could think of to get to know. It is full of excitement, twists and turns, unexpected endings. I never have to wonder if I will be there for me, if I will show up for me, if I will have enough time for me. I will always do all of these things. And that is my commitment to me. Bigger, more important, grander than any commitment I have ever made.

I saw the movie "Wonder Woman 1984" with my kids. When we came out they were excited about some parts and critiquing a few parts. When they looked over at me, I was in tears and confusion crossed their faces. What had happened? In the movie, I saw me. I saw who I am. I am rare, beautiful and powerful. I have the capacity inside of me to change my story, to heal myself, to bring this healing to others, to love, to be my best me. I felt my best me. I felt that I am unique with a beauty beyond measure, coupled with an ability to love, enabling me to thrive and shine and become. I didn't need to know in that moment that we are all given this. I just needed to know that this is me. I felt it and knew it and desired a life full of more than I could dream.

I LOVE MYSELF

Chapter 6

Mind chatter

W hat is my new mind chatter? I learned from the book to say repeatedly "I love you Janny". I took this to heart and it made all the difference. Later as I healed and learned to love myself, I realized there are more messages for me. My next message to myself was "I will always forgive you Janny, every time." Another message was "I meet my needs".

What do I want to hear? What needs do I want to meet? What hurts the most when someone else says it to me? What will I make my new recording say?

I fail to realize how much my mind is on a replay of pain, replay of lack, replay of trauma. My brain will literally replay a painful experience or trauma over and over and I won't even notice it. I will have no idea until I tune in to what I am thinking about that I was just reliving the past yet again. So what do I replace this pattern with?

I have chosen a feeling of abundance, of love. I tell myself this over and over again to feel the great abundance and pure love. I tell myself that I will never give up on me. No, not ever. God has already promised me that my tears will be wiped away and pain replaced with pure joy. I trust Him.

I have been taught that deep pains come from our childhood before the age of eight when our brains are in the programming stage. These pains cannot be fixed by anyone but me. Anything I try to mask this pain with will be temporary. I believe this and have seen it in my life. Whatever anyone else does is never enough. It might help for a little while but soon I am wanting more.

In order to get this hole in my heart filled I must love me and love me without restrictions. There is nothing I need to do to earn this love from myself. There are no rules, no standards. I want to fill the hole in my heart and I start with saying I love you Janny.

Then I begin to fill my heart with light and love. I send this light all throughout my body. This light, I feel it sweeping through every crevice, every intent, and every hidden place until there is nothing washing through me but light. This love that I feel cannot be described. It is just felt. Feel the light as it comes down from above, enters through the top of your head and finds its way to every part of your being.

Once this love is felt there is no going back. This feeling is so powerful, this light of purity, that darkness and sadness cannot survive when this light is present.

You might ask – "How do I feel this love? When do I feel this love? What if I can't feel this love?" I began with creating this feeling each day. I would imagine what it would feel like. For five minutes at first, then for ten. I did it while I was running, while I was driving, while I was sitting. It did not matter what this meditative period looked like – just that I tried.

I created this feeling, working to feel it. Then I would tuck the feeling away in my heart to have it to call back on throughout the day. As time went on, as I worked with different professionals to heal my trauma, as I used various apps and tools to learn to meditate, this feeling of love became my very best friend.

So give me your list of why you should be sad – give me the recording of your "life" with its plethora of problems. It is the list of why you should be sad to keep you living in lack. I have mine too! My painful list that would cause you to sit me down and ask me if I am forgetting what I have been through.

But the truth remains – we may feel joy in ANY circumstances. Any! Our circumstances do NOT dictate our joy.

As our mind chatter of stress, worry, past emotions, fear and problems is replaced with intentional thoughts to include feelings of happiness, joy, love, peace and hope – playing these new emotions each day - we attract this into our life as our energy is drawing this light towards us.

I have a new memorized emotion. This is where I live. I add new mind chatter that is just right for me. I am intentional with my mind. I love myself!

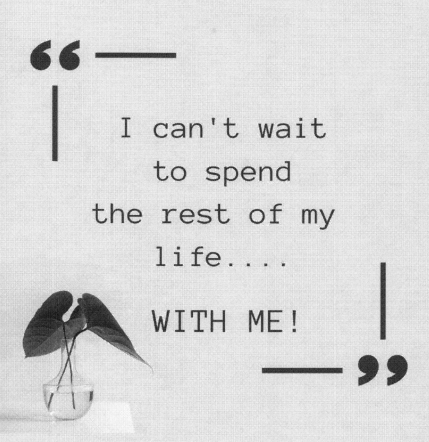

I can't wait
to spend
the rest of my
life....

WITH ME!

Chapter 7

Walk with God

I have known my Heavenly Father above since I was a very little girl. He taught me how much He loves me. He taught me to love myself, to see myself as He sees me. He showed me, as I began to feel love for myself, how much is ahead for me.

I feel very blessed to have always known my Heavenly Father's love and warmth in my life. We are all His children, His work and His glory. He is deeply invested in each of our lives. How everything works and all that goes on, it feels impossible to make sense of. He is inside of each of us. He has always been. When we are disconnected from ourselves, nothing makes sense.

I have learned through trial and error that I err when I try to give advice or tell anyone what to feel, what is real, what they should or should not do. Rather, I simply share my story. My story with God is amazing, incredible, and powerful. I have sat with Him, cried with Him, walked with Him. Answers have come from Him as I quiet my mind and listen, as I share my FEELINGS with Him. He gives me freedom to choose. He takes the decisions I make and creates miracles with them. God lives in me.

This book is a miracle for me. One day I went to the gym to work out. As I was leaving I had a thought come clearly to my mind that I would share my story, write a book. This was in 2015 when I was up to my eyeballs in stress and the needs from those in my family, my personal needs and my career were drowning me. There was absolutely no time to spare.

A few short weeks later I talked to a dear friend I had not spoken to in years. She shared her journey of writing books. I felt a desire to follow this path. I tucked this idea away in my heart. A few years later thoughts entered my mind again about writing. Little did I know that God was preparing my heart.

In February of 2020 a few people close to me joked about "my book" – a tender prayer in my heart that I had never shared with them. They literally asked me when my book was coming out. I felt hesitant. God told me it was time. I have learned to listen to Him. I have learned how much He shares with my heart, with my soul. In that moment the title came to me – Want More, Just Start. I had no idea where to start with my book then I laughed as God literally said – JUST START ☺

God whispered to me – I did not give you these experiences and this knowledge just for you. They are to be shared. I began to write, then other things longed for my attention and the project was set aside.

2022 was the year that this came to fruition. In June of 2022 I felt a deep desire to connect with my dear grandmother. I carved out three days and headed to her nursing home a short plane ride away. Our time together was sacred and is what inspired completion of my book. We cried together. I felt her tender heart weep as she shared how difficult it has been to now live in an assisted living home and have her sweetheart gone, he having passed away a year and a half ago.

She taught me strength. When he left, she did not. She still had love to give and lives to touch. Mine is one of them. We spoke of love, of loving ourselves. I cherish the memory of looking into my grandmother's eyes and seeing her, her seeing me and seeing her begin to more deeply see herself. We spoke of God. Her love for her Heavenly Father touched my heart. As we talked of what truly loving ourselves looks like she asked me to share with others the importance of this deep love and how to be our own best friend.

God is truly a personal God, a very personal God. We have personal lives with personal circumstances that need personal attention. So guess what? That is what He offers us, personal answers – simply ask Him!

Did I not speak peace to your heart? This is what He offers us. God is not the author of confusion.

I wrote a poem when I was 17 years old:

> Can confusion reign?
> I don't think it can.
> All will fall into place
> Know the Master's plan

His plan comes from Him to you for you.

I have been amazed at the miracles God has worked in my life. But then again, why should I be amazed because MIRACLES ARE WHAT HE DOES! God does not "owe" me a thing. He loves me, is aware of me, cherishes me deeply and gives good gifts.

He knows more than I know because He sees all. He asks me to trust Him and every time I do, with time I see why. Some things I do not get to see now, but He has shown me enough of the nows that later works for me too!

He will say in His loving way – "Janny, really???" I have proven myself to you soooo many times, will you simply trust me? And when in that moment the fears are too great and the pain too much – He holds space for me and sends His angels to surround me in love. His promises He has given me to my heart, heart to heart, spirit to spirit, are too beautiful to put into words. These feelings I cherish. These feelings I carry with me as my light. These feelings flood my being.

From infancy I was invited by my loving parents to talk with God, walk with God, to know that I am a child of God and I am loved by Him. This memorized emotion I am thankful for as it went deep into my soul and I have always known of the truth of His love.

I heard a phrase once that says – if you do not know something to be true, lean on others and their knowing until you come to know. I invite anyone to lean on my knowing, to lean on me. Many things in my life have been hard and thankfully faith was not one of them.

God has been the one who never leaves my side, never gives up on me, never withdraws but rather always accepts me exactly where I am at. He does it for all of us unconditionally. Sometimes we do not see it, cannot feel it, often simply because we cannot even feel ourselves.

I have had the beautiful sacred opportunity to get to know people who have not had this gift of feeling God's love but instead for one reason or another have felt distance from the love from their creator. As these trusting individuals have embarked on a journey of self-love, they began to feel God's love. This has been a gift to behold.

On April 10, 2020 I fasted with many across the world for the healing of our planet. On April 12, 2020 I asked God to heal the world in such a way that people would be brought to know Him, where people would not deny that He had His hand in this miracle of healing. Those that have eyes to see, let them see. Those that have ears to hear, let them hear. Will you see? Will you hear? This healing of our planet is occurring one individual at a time, one soul at a time, one choice at a time. I feel safe in God's love. I feel safe.

CAN CONFUSION REIGN?

I don't think it can

All will fall into place

Know the Master's Plan

Janny Tolman, 1992

Chapter 8

Meet my own needs

Parents raise their children hoping above all other hopes that they will be happy and well taken care of. Parents hope their children will make choices to bring lasting happiness and that their needs will be met. Children are taught to function in the society they live in and eventually meet their own needs. Needs include physical, emotional, mental, social and spiritual. Can I meet my own needs? What needs have I been ignoring?

More than once I have sat in loneliness. Many things over the years have brought this on. There were times I struggled with missing my cherished former spouse, wishing we were together and wishing I did not feel alone. I have sat missing my beloved sister who passed away, missing all of our best friend moments, wanting her with me and wanting someone to come and meet my needs. With these and other challenges I have felt alone. I wanted this connection to come back and my needs to be met. The feeling seemed to come more than go.

I was told that this feeling is a great teacher. What is it here to teach me? I pleaded with God to let me know what it was, to teach me so I could move on from the pain. I used the phrase so often of "letting go" and I had experienced this at various times in my life, but this was different. Something was tugging at my chest, something was going on.

I was ready to hear it, ready to go deep. Answers flooded my mind. This is what I felt was going on with me – I have a memorized emotion, deep in my computer brain, telling me that I need my needs met. What was wrong? This is what I had been thinking and living by - "I need to gain approval from another, convince another person what my needs are, for them to please agree that these needs must be met and then for this person to MEET MY NEEDS!" Somehow, someone – and the right Mr. Someone – would meet my needs.

Guess what I learned? I am not two years old, I am not six years old, I am not at the whim of another as they decide when and how my needs will be met. I am now an adult very capable of meeting my own needs. Not only capable of doing it but I will do it. I will meet my needs. I am the answer. Not him, not her, not them, not anyone. In fact, no one else can do this for me is what I was taught by my psychologist.

If I desire my needs to be fulfilled by someone else, I will with 100% certainty be left disappointed. I sit with myself asking myself with intention and sincerity - what are your needs Janny? Then – I MEET MY NEEDS! I don't need approval to move forward. I don't need anyone to agree that my needs matter or that my needs are real. They are real to me and now I meet my needs.

In order to meet my needs and know my needs, I must listen to my FEELINGS. I must want to truly value my feelings. I need to know that my feelings matter. There is someone to listen to me, hear me, and show up for me. When I listen to my own feelings, I am not lonely. I am not alone.

Let's go back to the example of children, to the children we want to have happiness. These children learn from what they see their parents/guardians do. When they get to watch a parent or guardian who loves them unconditionally, beams and radiates happiness AND meet their own needs – this will place them on their path of self-love.

I have observed many mothers (including myself) wearing an imaginary badge of pride declaring that their needs are not met because they are meeting their children's needs and putting their children first, taking care of the children's needs at their own expense. I am finding when I meet my needs, I have so much more to give as I have a reservoir that runneth over!

I am now in the process of truly honoring me and meeting my needs. My brain tries to talk me into getting someone else on board to agree with me that my needs matter. It is not necessary. I agree that my needs matter. I meet my needs.

How can
I show up
for ME
today?

Chapter 9

Answers lie within me

J ust start. Try something. Try anything. See what works. See what brings you to your true self, to know your true self, to be with you, to enjoy a sunset with you, to sit in peace and calm, feeling it throughout. This is what we want and hope for.

The vagus nerve goes from the crown of our head to the bottom of our feet. I allow myself to feel it. My parasympathetic nervous system lives in peace, rest, digest, repair and calm. When I get quiet with me, the answers lie within me. Before I could feel this I had to get out of my own way.

I needed validation from someone, anyone! Tell me I am right. Give me a stamp of approval. Help me feel validated.

And now, I gather information, listen, learn and go to me. Breathe. Feel. Listen to me.

The answers are all there. I trust myself, because I honor myself. I have gotten to know myself.

As I go deep, there is God. He has always been there. As I go deep, I feel me. I see me.

My meditation where I wrote and wrote and I sat and let words simply come to me and flow through me in a stream of consciousness ended up being all about my true self. My true self has been hidden by childhood trauma, generational trauma, masking my true self to try to fit in, unchosen habits that keep me in fight or flight.

In October of 2018 I decided to slow down and find me. It made no financial or logical sense. I was a divorced mother of four with my kids going back and forth between me and their father. I taught PE and we had finally received a raise so this income was much needed. I co-owned a small business that was growing, needing my attention. My psychologist told me I cannot help you if you don't slow your brain down. So it was time.

I applied for and was approved for FMLA (Family Medical Leave Act – an unpaid partial or full release from work for a short period of time to attend to personal or family medical needs) and went on my journey to find me, to find answers within me - those answers I had always sought. I was given approval to work part time with a substitute covering two or three days a week for five weeks.

With this time, I started on my path of finding me, giving myself permission to breathe, to feel. I talked to my sister and with her help I knew I would always look back on this time with gratitude that I chose me and gave me this gift. This has shown to be true. It honestly has shown to be more than true but invaluable.

When I was 16 I began writing poetry. Here is a simple poem I wrote and read now seeing I did not even comprehend how powerful and insightful these few short words are.

> Peace pray tell, where is it found?
> In my heart I look all around.
> Wait! What is this I see?
> Peace, it is inside of me!

I had made decisions through prayer, trusting God, trusting feelings from Him. Now it was time to slow down and trust me, and listen to me the "me" that was not capable before but could now slow down and listen. I found God and I are one.

This is your journey. Maybe you will find like me that gratitude is a tool you cannot live without, or like me that journaling is how you process and feel. Exercise has been my trusted companion to remove stress and invite many of those happy hormones! Many times each week I literally did run as I have always found I function better with exercise.

Another tool I use that helps greatly is looking at ME to see what needs changing or "fixing" rather than finding someone or something to blame outside of me. I felt when I did this I was headed in the right direction. I cannot forget my positive affirmations as I looked in the mirror and told myself with conviction all the wonderful things I was discovering about me and began to believe could be true about me!

If any gift of learning and healing that was given to me is helpful to you, I am humbled and grateful. If any part touches you, please share. Raise the energy, the healing, and the love. This is my prayer and my desire, the deepest desire of my heart, to give anything I can to help others.

I was taught each time I learned something new and wanted to help others that I first needed to help myself. Not only did I first need to help myself but I must release the intent that the main reason to help myself was so I could be ready to help others.

When I realized that I truly loved me, truly was doing this for me, it was when I said, with conviction, that if I walked this path and learned all I learned for me alone, it would have been worth every effort. At this point my light healed my own soul, my inner child knew she mattered. Now, I desire to share all I can, only this time it is different in that I share from this place of knowing the path, walking the path and continuing to walk this sacred path. Want more? Just start! When you are ready....

Peace pray tell, where is it found?

In my heart I look all around.

Wait! What is this I see?

Peace, it is inside of me.

Janny Tolman, 1992

Works cited

Lois Laynee: CEO and founder of Restorative Breathing – www.restoringbreathing.com

"Love Yourself Like Your Life Depends on It" by Kamal Ravikant

Thanks to Russell M. Nelson for the inspirational talk where I learned the meaning of metanoeo.

"We Can Do Better and Be Better" President Russell M Nelson, April 2019 address, The Church of Jesus Christ of Latter Day Saints

About Janny

How does one even write an "about me?"

So when I was little I always wanted to be a wife and a mother. I dreamed of love and loving. I played house and cared for my younger sisters with my big sister Kim. I watched my amazing mother and father. My dreams came true twice for the wife and four times for the mother! And so far, a bonus of 2 sweet grandbabies. If I am lucky, the third time is the charm, and the wife thing might just stick. ☺

When I am not with my amazing family, I get to do what I love and call it work.

I feel grounded in my children, grandbabies, sisters, parents, extended family, cherished friends, God, Jesus Christ, my career, my dreams, my passions, my past, my present, my future.

I will include my little tidbit below so you can say ooooooooooo, she is smart! But what is really me, is sitting down with whoever is in front of me, and seeing and feeling their best, most beautiful self just like I do with myself.

That's my version of the "about me."

Janny

Janny Tolman M.Ed., B.S., CA graduated from Arizona State University with a Master's Degree in Curriculum and Instruction. Her Bachelor's Degree is in Exercise Science. She holds a current teaching certificate in the state of Arizona, where she taught in Gilbert and Chandler for 16 years.

Janny has co-owned Ironwood Chiropractic since 2014 where she works with patients and continues to train and educate herself in different healing modalities, including a two-year-long neurosequencing practicum focusing on the brain and trauma. Her most prized education has come from the school of hard knocks.

Her passion has always been to be a conduit for others on their own life journeys.

If this book touched or helped you, you're going to want Janny's free tool to turn on your parasympathetic nervous system.

Visit **JannyTolman.com** to get started.

You can also email Janny at **Janny@JannyTolman.com** to get connected.

Made in the USA
Middletown, DE
12 November 2023

42481394R00044